I AM WHO GOD SAYS I AM

MAGS MUTIZWA

Published by:
R. H. Publishing
3411 Preston Road, Ste. C-14-146
Frisco, Texas, 75034

Copyright © 2018, Margaret Mutizwa

ISBN#978-1-945693-14-4

ENDORSEMENTS

Mags Mutizwa, in her new book, *I Am Who God Says I Am*, gives an unpretentious, yet insightful look into the scriptural principles referenced by her title. She uses personal examples and stories from her own experiences, as well as, testimonies from others to drive home these truths. The declarations and prayer that accompanies the end of each chapter, along with a place for personal notations, adds to the practical application of these insights. It's a perfect book to keep close at hand for those times of devotion when you need a reminder that you are who God says you are.

Susan Bozarth
Christ For The Nations Instructor, Speaker, Author

Mags Mutizwa has a unique love for God's people. *I AM WHO GOD SAYS I AM* comes out of that love, combined with a deep longing to see others set free and fulfill their God-given purpose. As you journey through this seven-day devotional, you will be blessed, refreshed and spiritually nourished.

Jo Naughton
Pastor Harvest Church, UK
www.jonaughton.com/healed-for-life

DEDICATION

I dedicate this book to my mother, Alice Nhekairo, a woman who introduced Jesus Christ to her family and changed the course of generations. She loved God and despite the difficult circumstances that surrounded her, she found strength and solace in Him. She taught me how to pray through good times and bad. She stood on the Word of God and overcame tough situations because of her faith in Jesus.

Thank you, Mum, for introducing us to Jesus Christ. I love and appreciate you, and I thank God for your life and for raising me to be a strong, prayerful woman of God.

ACKNOWLEDGMENTS

I would like to thank the following people who made this book possible for me in so many different and wonderful ways.

Thank you, Emmanuel Mutizwa, for supporting and encouraging me to seek God for his will for my life. Thank you for giving me the time and space to write this book.

Thank you, Mother Archbishop Eunor Guti. You have always encouraged me, even from the time I was a young girl, you even advised me which nursing major I should specialize in. You are my role model in the faith.

Thank you, Pastor Anne, my mentor. God sent you into my life at just the right time. Your time, counsel and words of encouragement have shaped me into the woman I am today. You have taught me that every battle is won on our knees in prayer.

Thank you to my District Pastors, Paul and Dr. Shylet Mukasa, for believing in me and supporting me.

Thank you, Professor Susan Bozarth, for encouraging me and believing in me. Your Christian Woman class transformed my mindset as a woman in a great way, I enjoyed your counselling class (STOP IT) and most of all the Joshua and Judges class has taught me a lot about leadership.

Thank you, Matina Newsom, for the book club you started in 2015/16 and all the time you spent helping me edit this book.

Thank you, Chipo Shiloh Moyo, for your encouragement and assistance in making this book a reality.

Thank you, Mom, Pastor Epiphania Mutizwa for encourging me and standing with me in prayer through everything. I love and appreciate you.

Thank you to all my good friends who helped me in so many different ways, working behind the scenes—Ruwa, Terri, Charity, Tomika, Karen, Mo, Abz, Nomsa, Monique, Miriam, Mbuya Pam, Jolomi, Tsitsi, Ros, Brian, Emily, Noma, Pamela, Shantell, Mandi, Primrose, Nyaradzo, Edwina, Loveness, and Matt and Hanna for the 5-star photo shoot.

I would also like to thank members of the Victory prayer group—Mama Caroline, Daniela and Salifu for your support and prayers.

I cannot say thank you enough. All I can say is to God be the Glory, and may He give you Divine help in your endeavors, as well.

TABLE OF CONTENTS

FOREWORD

As I read, *I AM WHO GOD SAYS I AM*, I could not help but think about your life and how far you have come in the things of God. All of us experience events in our lives that can discourage us and shake us up. The only way to grow and mature during these times is to do what you are instructing the reader to do in your book.

Unless we know, I mean really know, who we are in Christ, the road can and will be a tough one. However, when we believe the Word and keep our hearts and minds focused on it and the Lord Himself, we will always come out on top. Victory in Jesus!

I pray for all who read this book and follow the daily declarations that your life will be changed—renewed—so you can fulfill all that God has call you to do. You can do all things through Christ because you are who God says you are

Archbishop Dr. Eunor Guti
Forward In Faith Ministries International
www.fifmi.org

I am delighted to write this foreword, not only because Pastor Mags Mutizwa has been a friend and a close associate for more than eight years, but also because I believe we need to work on knowing our self-worth, rather than increasing our "self-esteem."

When we focus on developing self-esteem, we work on being better at various things such as, losing weight, thinking more positively, changing careers, increasing our earnings. All of these are good, but what happens when we place our entire value in them? What happens when those "good" things change or disintegrate?

Our value disintegrates right along with it. I have seen so many people who have gotten caught in this trap—never seeing themselves through the eyes of the Lord. They conclude they have absolutely no value and believe they never will.

Revealed in this book is a specific message that is very important for us all.

"I am who God says I am," means that I am of great worth, no matter what I think, feel, or do, whether I "succeed" or "fail," that core knowledge does not change. Even though I feel the pain of failure, if I have self-worth, I still know I am valuable and "good."

So, hopefully, that includes you! Your personal awakening to the importance of this message and the release of its astonishing power might constitute something of a revolution in your life. You may begin to do things and achieve goals you never imagined were possible for you in your previously, limited understanding of your self-worth.

So make a life-changing decision today. Buy this inspirational book and begin to live a life that truly matters.

Anne Salu MSc, FHEA, MBCS
Senior Lecturer
Anglia Ruskin University, London, UK

INTRODUCTION

My first year at Christ For The Nations Bible Institute in Dallas, Texas, was tough. God began to deal with me personally, bringing up hurt and pain from the past that I had swept under the carpet. I said to the Lord, "I am at a Bible School. I am here to learn how to minister to others. Why are you now dealing with me?"

As the months and years (3 years) went by, I began to appreciate the inward work God was doing. I found out that I needed Christ on a daily basis. I found that without Him, I have and I am nothing. But most of all, I learned that my identity was in Christ alone. My identity is not in my career, friends, spouse, achievements or failures. My true identity is in who God says I am.

The Bible says in Psalm 119:130,
"The unfolding of your words gives light,
It imparts understanding to the simple" (ESV).

I began to search the Scriptures to discover what God says about me, and I found my identity in His Word.

This 7-Day devotional is designed to give you the same confidence I found in 'knowing' who you are in Christ. If you have felt rejected, abandoned, unloved, overlooked, and unappreciated, or if you have gone through a divorce, or suffer from low self-esteem, this book is for you.

When I was in Bible school as a scholarship student, in one semester I went from being the President's office student

15

assistant to being on the janitorial staff. I thank God He had been teaching me that my Identity is in Him, not what I do; hence I enjoyed the janitorial assignment. I could have felt rejected or less than, but I knew that who I was, was not determined by the job or position assigned to me, but in Christ Jesus.

At the end of each chapter or day, are daily confessions. These are very important, and not just for that day only. Speak them out loud over yourself. Copy and paste them onto your wall if you want.

The Bible says in Proverbs 18:21, "Death and life are in the power of the tongue." Begin to speak life—declare daily who God says you are, until your soul (your mind, will and emotions) believes and is renewed and transformed with the Word of God.

Try to complete this over the seven-day period. Write down your thoughts and take notes on a daily basis in the space provided for you. Consider how this chapter has spoken to you and in which areas you now see the truth and want to take to reach a different destination.

The good thing about God's Word is it never loses its power. So, even when you have completed this, if you feel discouraged or are experiencing a set-back in some area, get it out and read it again. It will produce the same rewards as it first did. Why? Because the truth is still the truth. And the truth is: You are the apple of God's eye. He loves you and has your name written on the palm of His hand. You are more than a conqueror through Christ Jesus, which means you are victorious in Him.

" The facts of who you seem to be are not necessarily a reflection of the truth of who you are. "

Ginger Lindsay

You are who God says you are!

Chapter 1

YOU ARE LOVED

Have you have felt unloved, rejected, unworthy, unimportant, unlovable or even not pretty enough? This reminds me of a story I read.

Many years ago, before the sensitive and politically correct society in which we live today, there was a boy who was continually in trouble. He was forever breaking the rules and always getting into trouble at school. His father could not understand why. He provided for him in every way with a good home, he spent time with him fishing and going to his ballgames, and he showered him with unconditional love, but the father couldn't figure out why the boy wouldn't mind.

He had been raised in church and had even been in Sunday school for five years. His father was consistently reading the Bible to him, and his father had never provoked him to anger. His son's behavior was a mystery to him.

One day when his son was upstairs playing around with his baseball, which he'd been told repeatedly not to do, he ended up breaking one of his bedroom windows. The boy was ten year's old and knew better because his father had told him time and again to not play ball in the house. The father headed upstairs and took off his belt. The boy knew what was coming so he voluntarily bent over and kneeled next to his bed.

But the father said, "Son, here, take this belt." Which

his son did. Then his father took off his shirt and kneeled down on the bed and said, "Son, I want you to give me seven lashes with this belt across my back."

His son started to cry and said that he couldn't do it. His father kept insisting until the son finally relented and started hitting his father across the back with the belt, but it wasn't hard enough.

He said, "Harder son, harder!"

When the boy finally lashed the belt across his father's back seven times with greater force, the father asked him, "Son, do you know why I had you do this?"

The son said, "No."

The father said, "When Jesus went to the cross for us, He took the worst punishment that has ever been inflicted upon any man. He was pummeled, He was beaten, His beard was plucked out, and He was punished like no one has ever been punished. Who do you really think did this to Jesus?"

The boy, still whimpering, hesitated and finally said he thought it was the Jews or the Romans, but the boy's father said, "No, it was God the Father Who punished Jesus for everything that we have ever done wrong and or will ever do wrong in the future (Isaiah 52:14, 15; 53:1-12). He took the punishment that He didn't deserve to save those who didn't deserve saving. That is how much the Father and Jesus loved us" (John 3:16). It was God's love most gloriously displayed for us who deserved His wrath.

The boy was shaken deeply by this lesson and from that day forward, he never seemed to get into the same amount of trouble again … not perfect, but changed. Maybe it was because he wasn't sure how his dad would react again. The boy didn't ever want to use the belt on his dad again; although the father never said anything more about it. Whatever is was, the message of God's love displayed on the cross by Christ forever changed this young man, and it has forever changed us. The boy was not perfect after that, by no means, but neither are we after being saved, but that doesn't take away what was accomplished at the cross.

Jesus gave his life on the cross for you because of His love for you. You did not do anything to deserve it, if anything like the young man in the story you broke the rules, rebelled and disobeyed God. Despite all that, according to John 15:13, "Greater love has no one than this, that someone lay down his life for his friends."

The father had done no wrong, but he took the punishment that was meant for his son. God sent His Son Jesus Christ to the earth to die for yours and my sin, the greatest act of love. You cannot do anything to buy it, work for it, or earn it—it is freely given.

I remember growing up in Africa my father owned grocery stores. One day, I accidentally started a fire in the back of the store which damaged a lot of property, and we lost a lot of stock in this fire. My father was angry for a moment, but he did not disown me as his child; he continued providing for me and caring for me despite the great loss I had caused his business. I was still his daughter, he continued to show me a father's love.

Quit listening to your critics and the people who make

you feel unworthy, or say you are a nobody, worthless or undesirable. The King of Kings and the Lord of lords left His throne in glory because you are so worth it. John 3:16 says, "For God so loved the world that He gave his only begotten son, that whosoever believes in Him should not perish but have eternal life."

The Creator of the universe gave His only Son to die for you, because of His unending and everlasting love for you. All you have to do is believe in Him and believe on His Word and you can experience and live in the fullness of His love. No one can take this love away from you.

In 1 John 4:18, 19, it states, "There is no fear in love. But perfect love drives out fear, because fear has to do with punishment. The one who fears is not made perfect in love. We love because he first loved us."

I encourage you not to live in fear. Do not think that one day He will not love you or change His mind about you. Human beings can change their mind about you in the same day—wait within the same hour. The same people who were laying palms at Jesus' feet on Palm Sunday saying, "Blessed is He Who cometh in the name of the Lord," were the same people a few days later who were shouting, "Crucify Him." So, if people can change their minds about Jesus, Who knew no sin, how much more can people love us and dislike us, too?

The good news is we have the assurance that God loves us just as we are. He does not require you to perform for His love. Just like the father in this story took the punishment instead of his son to show him how much he loved him. People will ask you to jump through hoops and do a, b, c and d to earn their love, but God, in all His majesty, in all His infinite wisdom loves you for you. He loves you the way He created you, and you do not have to out-perform anyone to gain or earn His love. It is a free gift.

I do not know what has happened in your life that may cause you to feel unloved or unworthy. However, I want you to know that you are loved by God Himself. He formed you in your mother's womb, according to Jeremiah 1:5, "Before I formed you in the womb I knew you, before you were born I set you apart."

You were not a mistake, God knew you and has a plan and a purpose for your life. Do not listen to the voice of the enemy that tells you that you are a mistake. Even if your parents told you that you were not planned, God's Word says that He formed you before you were in your mothers' womb. If people have said, "No one loves you; no one cares for you," read this Scripture out loud and proclaim it over yourself: "God formed me before I was in my mothers' womb, and He set me apart!"

The International Bible version says in Psalm 8:4, "What is man that you take notice of him, or the son of man that you pay attention to him?" Another translation says that, "You are mindful of him, and that you care for him." People may have said, "Don't mind her; don't pay him any attention." One Who is greater than any man notices you. He pays attention to you. God cares for you, and He has you on His mind.

You might have been let down by a parent, family member, spouse, boyfriend or girlfriend or even people in the church. They do not have the final say over your life—God does—and He is not finished with you yet. The God of Heaven and Earth, the only true God, Who created you, has not changed His mind about you. He loved you on the cross, and He still loves you today. Hold your head up high child of God, and start every day from today knowing you are loved by God.

Write down any labels people have put on you or lies of the devil that have caused you to feel unloved. Then put a big cross over them because that is not who you are.

I heard a sermon illustration about the chemical reaction that happens to a cake when the ingredients are mixed up and it is baked in the oven. There is no way you can separate the eggs, flour, oil and sugar after it is baked. This is how the love of God is to you. Nothing and no one can separate you from the Love of God.

DAY 1   DECLARATIONS

I am loved by God
God formed me in my mother's womb
I am fearfully and wonderfully made
I am the apple of God's eye
I am set apart
God has me on His mind
Nothing can separate me from the Love of God
I am loved by The Almighty God, Who created the heavens and
the earth

PRAYER

Dear God, I thank You for loving me so much that You died on
the cross for my sins. I thank You for creating me just as I am
and loving me despite all my faults, failures and weaknesses.
I thank You for setting me apart in my mother's womb, and I
thank You for reminding me that I am loved by You and Your
love is better than the love of man. Help me to walk in, and
experience Your love every day. In Jesus' name. Amen.

NOTES

Chapter 2

YOU ARE FORGIVEN

"Jesus has already been scourged for your sins so why beat yourself up?" Pastor Jo Naughton.

Has the enemy or people ever made you feel like your past is so bad that you are beyond receiving forgiveness? Has the enemy made you rehearse your past and make you feel like what you did is unforgivable or you will have to work or buy forgiveness? The Word of God says, "In whom we have redemption through his blood, the forgiveness of sins, according to the riches of his grace."

The Trokosi system is an illegal, traditional religious practice found in parts of Ghana, Benin and Togo. The Trokosi practice plays an important part in the rural justice system. When a crime is committed, the fetish priest consults the gods to ascertain which family has committed the crime. In order to atone for the crime, that family will have to provide a virgin girl to serve at the shrine. Otherwise, the Ewe people believe, deaths and misfortunes will be visited on the family.

The Trokosi girl now belongs to the gods, and therefore, the priest. She is effectively a slave, expected to do the hard labor for the priest without receiving any payment or even food. As a 'wife' to the gods, she will also sleep with the god. It is believed the god visits the girl in the form of the priest. Girls may be expected to serve a set number of years, or there may be a generational contract whereby every time a Trokosi woman dies in the shrine, someone else from the family must replace her and serve for life.

The practice was made illegal in Ghana in 1998. As a mother or a father, could you imagine giving up your child, who you raised from birth, to a priest to appease the gods? All the sleepless nights you had, the diaper changes, the dreams and aspirations you had for her are now gone because of your sin?

Thank God for Jesus Christ. God sent His one and only Son to die for your sins, so you would not have to sacrifice your family anymore. He was the sacrificial Lamb for your transgressions. In the Old Testament, livestock—goats, sheep, and cows to name a few, were sacrificed for the atonement of sin. There might not be any livestock worldwide if this practice was still in place. The Bible says in 1 Peter 3:18, "For Christ also suffered once for sins, the righteous for the unrighteous, that he might bring us to God, being put to death in the flesh but made alive in the spirit" (ESV).

In 1 John 2:2, it also tells us, "He is the propitiation for our sins, and not for ours only but also for the sins of the whole world" (ESV). Propitiation means an offering to appease (satisfy) an angry, offended party. In 1 John 2:2 and 4:10 it clearly explains that it is Christ's atoning blood that appeases God's wrath, on all confessed sin. By the sacrifice of Himself, Jesus Christ provided the ultimate / hilasmós ("propitiation"). This is the propitiation for our sins, and not for ours only, but also for the sins of the whole world.

The Word of God also tells us in the Book of Romans 3:23-25, "For all have sinned and fall short of the glory of God, and are justified freely by His grace through the redemption that is in Christ Jesus. God presented Him as an atoning sacrifice through faith in His blood, in order to demonstrate His righteousness, because in His forbearance He had passed over the sins committed beforehand."

It doesn't matter what you have done; Jesus Christ paid the price for your sin on the cross and there is nothing you could have done to earn forgiveness. He gave it to you by His grace. Unlike the tribe mentioned above, you do not have to sacrifice anyone or yourself. Forgiveness was freely given on the cross. Instead of you suffering for your own sin or dying for your own sin, Jesus took your place, and He was the acceptable sacrifice as He knew no sin Himself, but He became sin on the cross that you and I can experience His love and forgiveness. You can walk free from guilt and condemnation because the blood of Jesus Christ paid it all.

"The only sin that is a problem is unconfessed sin."
Pastor Jo Naughton

All you have to do is confess your sin, ask God to forgive you and receive His love and forgiveness. He already went to the cross so you do not have to. What do I mean by you do not have to go to the cross? The cross is a painful place; the cross is an isolated place. Even Simon Peter, who was close to Jesus, denied knowing him on the way to the cross.

Jesus suffered on the cross and was pierced in His side and died on the cross. You no longer have to suffer or be tortured or tormented for your sin. Jesus paid it all for you on the cross, He did not do a half job. He did a complete job. That is why He declared, "It is finished." Do not allow the enemy to sow lies in your thoughts that what you have done is beyond redemption, and you must pay for it all your life. Do not let the enemy or people limit you from walking in your inheritance or the fullness of your calling based on your past.

Jesus said it is finished—you have to receive, believe, embrace His forgiving power and walk free. You are no longer a slave to fear or sin. You are a child of God, bought by the precious blood of the Lamb. If you have never asked God for forgiveness or asked Him to come into your life, please say the prayer on the last page, and you can walk in this forgiveness from this moment.

I encourage you to walk with confidence, knowing that you are released from your past. God does not hold it against you. You don't have to sacrifice anything because He already paid the full price for you.

SOURCE: https://vimeo.com/65521460

PROPITIATION: http://biblehub.com/greek/2434.htm;
Trokosi: slave to the gods from fjona hillPLUS4 years ago

DAY 2   DECLARATIONS

I am forgiven
I am redeemed
I am no longer a slave to fear, sin or my past
I am free in Jesus Christ
I am no longer identified by my past
I have a new identity in Jesus
I am His child—bought by the precious blood of Jesus
I AM FORGIVEN

PRAYER

Dear Lord, thank You for dying on the cross for my sins. Thank You for forgiving me for _____. (You can list what you have been forgiven for). Thank You, Lord, for setting me free, according to Your Word that says in John 8:36, "If the Son therefore shall make you free, ye shall be free indeed." I thank You that I am free. I am loved by the King of kings, and I am forgiven. No more bondage, no more chains, no more condemnation, I am free in Christ Jesus Who purchased my sins on the cross. Thank You, Lord. In Jesus' name, Amen.

NOTES

Chapter 3

YOU ARE RESTORED

Have you ever felt like there are limits on your life because of your past mistakes, where you were born, or how you were raised? Does the enemy make you think you can never achieve what others have achieved? Do you feel you can only go so far, and no further because of your past, what you did or what was done to you?

The last couple of days have taught us that we are loved and forgiven by God. The good news does not end there—you are also Restored. In the Book of 2 Samuel, chapter 9, we learn about Mephibosheth. Here is a recap of this amazing story: "When God had removed Saul, he raised up David to be their king, of whom he testified and said, 'I have found in David the son of Jesse a man after my heart, who will do all my will'" (Acts 13:22).

When David finally became king over all Israel, he inquired if there were any left of Saul's house or family by saying, "Is there still anyone left of the house of Saul, that I may show him kindness for Jonathan's sake?" (2 Samuel 9:1). He sent for Mephibosheth.

"Then King David sent and brought him from the house of Machir the son of Ammiel, at Lo-debar, and Mephibosheth the son of Jonathan, son of Saul, came to David and fell on his face and paid homage. David said, 'Mephibosheth!' He answered, 'Behold, I am your servant.' David said to him, 'Do not fear, for I will show you kindness for the sake of your father Jonathan, and I will restore to you all the land of Saul your father, and you shall eat at my table always.' And he paid homage and said, 'What is your servant, that you should show regard for a dead dog such as I?'" (2 Samuel 9:5-8).

Notice the humility of Mephibosheth. In one of the kindest acts in all of Israel's history, David said "All that belonged to Saul and to all his house I have given to your master's grandson, and you and your sons and your servants shall till the land for him and shall bring in the produce, that your master's grandson may have bread to eat, but Mephibosheth your master's grandson shall always eat at my table" (2 Samuel 9:9b, 10).

Mephibosheth was crippled when his nurse dropped him as they fled the palace when King Saul died. She was meant to protect him, but he fell and was lame in his feet (2 Samuel 4:4). Mephibosheth was only five years old when this happened. At that time, he could walk, run and play like any other five-year-old, but all that changed the day he was dropped.

He was the king's grandson, he had servants, and access to everything at his fingertips, but in one day, he lost everything. He went from luxury to living in a poor place and being dependent on his nurse for everything.

David sought him out and brought him back to the palace. He Restored him to his place as the grandson of the king. Once again, he had servants waiting on him. David did not just give him lodging somewhere in the kingdom where he could be looked after and just have a better life. He gave him a place at the kings table and his grandfathers' land was given to him. Overnight, Mephibosheth became royalty again. He was still lame in his legs, but he was no longer living in poverty. He now owned land and sat at the highest table in the kingdom.

What has crippled you? Sin? Abuse? Physical or sexual abuse? Abandonment, divorce, failure? Jesus Christ is calling you to come to Him as you are, and He will restore you to your rightful place. Like Mephibosheth, David did not hold his grandfather's sin against him.

Mephibosheth was treated like the king's son; he was accepted graciously at the king's table. He was able to be in the king's presence, and he was provided all that he needed, even though he was lame. Mephibosheth couldn't even provide for his own living. That was us before we were saved. Now, we can dine at the Lord's Table.

The Bible says in Mathew 11:28, "Come to me, all you who are weary and burdened, and I will give you rest."

Jesus calls you to come unto Him, not to carry the weight of sin, your past or any burden you have. He says He will give you rest.

In Joel 2:25, 26, it says, "I will restore to you the years that the swarming locust has eaten, the hopper, the destroyer, and the cutter, my great army, which I sent among you. You shall eat in plenty and be satisfied, and praise the name of the Lord your God, who has dealt wondrously with you. And my people shall never again be put to shame" (ESV).

When Mephibosheth sat at the king's table, any visitors

that came and did not know his past, saw him as any other royal person at the table. I don't think Mephibosheth would announce to those at the table, "Hello, I am Mephibosheth. I am lame." He didn't need to. His identity was one of royalty, and so is yours as a son or daughter of the King of kings. He does not treat you according to your past failures, what you did or what was done to you. You are part of the family. Quit seeing yourself as unworthy or unqualified. Quit announcing yourself by your past failures or mistakes. You are not who they say you are. You are who God says you are.

Isaiah 61:7 says, "Instead of your shame there shall be a double portion; instead of dishonor they shall rejoice in their lot; therefore in their land they shall possess a double portion; they shall have everlasting joy" (ESV).

There is a seat for you at the King's table. You are worth it—you deserve it. Not because of what you have done, but because of His love, forgiveness and restoration for you.

God does not hold our old sins against us, nor does He act like forgiveness is a favor to us, even though it is. When President Lincoln was asked how he would treat the rebellious southerners when they were defeated, he said, "I will treat them as if they had never been away." And that is how God treats us.

You cannot change your past, but with God, you can change your future. God can heal, deliver, and restore you from past abuse, sin, divorce, or anything that causes you to feel like you are not worthy of a good future. The Bible says in James 1:17, "Every good gift and every perfect gift is from above, and cometh down from the Father of lights, with whom is no variableness, neither shadow of turning."

Jeremiah 32:27 says, "Behold, I am the Lord, the God of all flesh. Is anything too hard for me?"

Nothing is too hard for our God. He can heal all your hurt and pain and restore you to fullness of life, so you can live the abundant life that He wants you to have.

John 10:10 says, "The thief comes only to steal and kill and destroy. I came that they may have life and have it abundantly."

The devil has tried all he can to kill and destroy you. You may have been abused as a child and feel like that's your life-long identity. You think you can never love or be loved because of that breakup or divorce or sin. Jesus came that you may have life and have it abundantly.

The definition for abundant is: properly all-around, "more than" ("abundantly"); beyond what is anticipated, exceeding expectation; "more abundant," going past the expected limit ("more than enough . . .").

Christ wants you to live an abundant, more than, life. He wants you to experience beyond what you have anticipated. He wants to exceed your expectations; therefore, He desires you to walk in Restoration and not be limited by your past.

Like Mephibosheth, He is inviting you to the King's table. You are a prince, you are a princess—the past does not matter anymore. You are Restored in Christ Jesus.

SOURCES:
From a sermon by David Rumley, *Redefining Lost*, 10/28/2009

QUOTES:
https://www.sermoncentral.com/illustrations/sermon-illustration-sermon-central-staff-quotes-restoration-74065? ref=TextIllustrationSerps
http://biblehub.com/greek/4053.htm - abundant definition

DAY 3   DECLARATIONS

I am Restored
I am no longer a product of my past failures
I am the son/daughter of the King of kings
There is room for me at the King's table
I am worth it
I am wonderfully and fearfully made
I will fulfill all that God created me to fulfill
I am who God says I am

PRAYER

Dear God, thank You for dying on the cross that I may experience abundant life. I thank You for restoring all the years I have lost because I did not realize who I really was in You. Forgive me for not expecting Your best for me. Forgive me for settling for less than Your best for me. Thank You for restoring me. I accept and expect the goodness of the Lord in my life. Thank You, Jesus, for covering my past in the blood and giving me a new start in You. In Jesus' name. Amen

NOTES

Chapter 4

YOU ARE ACCEPTED

Have you ever suffered rejection? Have you ever been in a group of people but still felt like you were out of place and did not belong? I know how this feels all too well. My sister was a School Prefect, which is a leadership position given to hardworking and responsible students in the final year of primary school and high school. I was always in the top class and excelled in creative writing, tennis and swimming. The day the Prefects were chosen, my name was not among the list. I was so hurt and disappointed. I had waited seven years of primary school only to be rejected.

I continued to excel in Tennis. I won the final tournament and was supposed to receive the tennis trophy at the end of the year. I was not awarded the trophy. I did not understand why? I asked my teacher and she told me, "Some of the teachers do not like you."

In retrospect, I do not think that was wise for this particular teacher to be so blunt with me. I felt more rejected than ever, and I felt that no one liked me or accepted me at this school. I carried this rejection with me to high school. I strived to be the best student. I stayed behind after classes to help my teachers. While others had fun in class and socialized, I would be the most attentive and the teachers' pet.

I joined every committee that I could, and helped in

41

the school shop during break time, while the others just simply enjoyed being young and free. All this hard work paid off because in my final year I was elected by the teachers' board to not only a Prefect position, but the Head Girl. (The Head Girl sits on the teachers' board on behalf of the students and is responsible for delegating tasks to the Prefects.) I had a different uniform than everyone in the school. I felt I had arrived, I felt I had received the acceptance I missed out on in primary school.

However, that title was not enough for me. I still suffered the rejection from my primary school. I may have been accepted by the High School teachers, but the Primary School teachers did not know who I really was. Inside me was a 12-year-old girl, striving for acceptance, even after receiving the position I strived for.

I remember baking a cake and taking it to my primary school teachers. I went with my school uniform and my fancy blazer (jacket) with the defined Head Girl trimming and my bright yellow Head Girl badge, so all the teachers that had rejected me, all the teachers who denied me the tennis cup, could see that I had finally made it. I wanted to show them that other teachers saw in me what they failed to see when I was a student there. I remember one teacher showed me she was really surprised by my achievement. She said that she was happy for me. I did not really take notice of their reactions. I just wanted them to know I found people who accepted me and have seen the value within me.

God loves you with an everlasting love, and He accepts you just the way you are. There is no need to perform for His acceptance. There is no need to work for Him to accept you. Having faced rejection in my primary school, I went out of my way to gain acceptance from the teachers. Maybe, if I had just been myself and enjoyed my high school years, I might still have been chosen as the Head Girl; however, because I let the rejection from primary school become my identity, I worked overtime and gave up certain opportunities to ensure I was given the Head Girl title.

Ephesians 1:6, states, "To the praise of the glory of his grace, wherein he hath made us accepted in the beloved." Another version, the NET Bible says, "To the praise of the glory of his grace that he has freely bestowed on us in his dearly loved Son." You are freely accepted in Christ Jesus, not of your own strength, work or effort, but through Jesus Christ.

Colossians 1:21, 22 says, "Once you were alienated from God and were enemies in your minds because of your evil behavior. But now he has reconciled you by Christ's physical body through death to present you holy in his sight, without blemish and free from accusation."

You have been reconciled to God through Christ. Your past and your sin is no longer held against you. You don't have to pay for your sins. Jesus paid it all. You do not have to labor to be reconciled to God. You are accepted in Him through Christ Jesus. Everyone has experienced rejection at some point in their lives. Yours could have been from a parent who felt you could never do good or they compared you to your siblings or peers. A friend rejected you, or maybe it was a boss who never appreciated your hard work. It could be a spouse. You may have experienced divorce or separation. It could simply be other people always get preferential treatment instead of you.

Mephibosheth, who we read about on day 3, was accepted by David as he was. He did not say, "Oh no, he is now lame; let me look for another person to show kindness to." He accepted him as he was and gave him the royal treatment. You need to come to God as you are with your broken past, rejection and pain. He does not require you to change who you are first. His love and forgiveness will restore you. His arms are open wide for you.

Like the prodigal son in Luke 15:11-32. He demanded his inheritance and went and squandered it in riotous living. However, when all the money was gone, he came to his senses and returned home. He was just going to ask for a servants' part because he thought his father would not accept him as his son due to his bad decisions. However, this is what his father said when he returned. "But the father said to his servants, 'Quick! Bring the best robe and put it on him. Put a ring on his finger and sandals on his feet. Bring the fattened calf and kill it. Let's have a feast and celebrate. For this son of mine was dead and is alive again; he was lost and is found'" (Luke 11:22-24). So they began to celebrate.

Do not wait another minute. Do not try to straighten out your life first before you come to God. He loves you and accepts you as you are. Just come to Him with your whole heart. Like the prodigal son, when you come to Jesus, He will not treat you like a servant or a second-class citizen. He accepts you as His son or daughter.

There is a song that says, "I am accepted by the one who matters most." It is comforting to know that the One true God, Who breathed life into you, accepts you.

Romans 8:37-39 says, "No, in all these things we are more than conquerors through him who loved us. For I am sure that neither death nor life, nor angels nor rulers, nor things present nor things to come, nor powers, nor height nor depth, nor anything else in all creation, will be able to separate us from the love of God in Christ Jesus our Lord."

Nothing can separate you from God's love for you. Dr. Mike Massa, a professor at Christ For The Nations Institute in Dallas says, "What Jesus did for you on the cross is stronger than what you have done or what was done to you." His love for you is stronger than your past or any hurt you incurred along the way.

That is the power of the acceptance of Christ. It is through His blood that you are accepted. Quit trying to stress yourself by going over and beyond your ability. Relax, take a deep breath enjoy your life in Christ. Stop planning and scheming ways to gain acceptance from people.

There is One Who sits on the Throne of Glory. He looks down and is pleased with you—just as you are. He does not like you better if you are a certain size, your hair is a certain length or color, you have bulging muscles and a six pack, your financial status, or you drive the best car. These are the acceptance standards of man. He loves you for you. He loves you for who you are inside and not your outward appearance. He accepts you as you are.

45

SOURCES:
Read more: http://www.whatchristianswanttoknow.com/bible-verses-about-love-25-awesome-scripture-quotes/ #ixzz4k2q8pKYq
https://www.openbible.info/topics/accepted_in_the_beloved

Day 4   Declarations

I am accepted by God
I am accepted just as I am
I do not have to work for his love and acceptance
I am created in the image of God
I am the apple of His eye
I am who God says I am

PRAYER

Dear Heavenly Father, thank You for accepting me just as I am. Forgive me for trying to win Your love and approval through my own limited efforts. Help me to walk in the peace and confidence that I am accepted by the One Who matters the most. In Jesus' name. Amen.

NOTES

Chapter 5

YOU ARE CHOSEN

Rhonda's eyes teared up as she shared her adoption story in Café Brazil. At 19 years old, Rhonda discovered by accident that the man she thought her entire life was her father, was in fact, not her biological father. Her real father had abandoned her when she was a baby due to a life of drugs and crime. Soon after, her mother married the man Rhonda came to know as her father. This man not only adopted Rhonda, but her younger brother, as well. He cared for them as if they were his own. This is why she didn't know the truth.

Rhonda felt hurt that her biological father was not there when she said her first words or helped her with her first steps. However, she was flooded with love for her adopted dad. She decided to write him a letter, explaining that she had found out the truth, but still loved him as her own dad. She was so grateful that he had given them the great upbringing they had received.

When she was younger, on a few occasions, some individuals had said to her, "Your father is not your real father." She would ask him about it, and he would ask her, "Does it really matter?"

She answered back, "No."

Then he would say, "Then it does not really matter!"

Rhonda's dad chose to adopt these two children as his own, despite the discouragement he received from friends and family. He loved them like they were his own.

Jesus Christ chose you before the foundation of the world. It does not matter where you came from or where you have been. He chose you—yes, you!

The day Rhonda and her brother were adopted, their lives changed forever. Their adopted father treated them like his own and even spoiled them in a good way. God's Word says in Ephesians 1:3, 4,

"Blessed be the God and Father of our Lord Jesus Christ, who has blessed us in Christ with every spiritual blessing in the heavenly places, even as he chose us in him before the foundation of the world, that we should be holy and blameless before him. In love."

The Bible also says in John 15:16, "You did not choose me, but I chose you and appointed you that you should go and bear fruit and that your fruit should abide, so that whatever you ask the Father in my name, he may give it to you."

You may have gone through a phase in your life where other people were chosen, but you were left out. You may feel others deserved to be chosen because of their background, education or even their looks. The good news for you is God chose you, exactly the way you are.

Just like Rhonda and her brother were chosen, you were chosen by God and welcomed into His family. John 15:16 says, "You did not choose me (God), but He chose you first.

In 1 John 4:19 we read, "We love God because He first loved us."

Do not live your life condemned or insecure about who

you are or used to be. God knows all you've done, but He still chose you. Accept His love, embrace His love and believe in your heart that He loved you. He died for you, and He chose you by name. Yes, you.

Isaiah 43:1 says, "But now thus says the Lord, he who created you, O Jacob, he who formed you, O Israel: 'Fear not, for I have redeemed you; I have called you by name, you are mine.'"

You are accepted into his family—everything that is His is yours, and all the promises in the Word of God belong to you. The same way Rhonda and her brother were chosen and adopted into a new family, you too, have been adopted into the family of God.

A good example is a household that has servants, maids, or butlers, their role is to work for the family and help them cook, serve food, clean the house and babysit the children. They do not receive the same treatment as the Children. I grew up in a house with a housemaid, and sometimes we had two. We lived under the same roof, and ate the same food. However, they were there to help my parents, for wages, even though my parents treated them with love and respect.

I had advantages as a daughter that they did not have. For example, my parents paid for my education, and bought me clothing. I had a bicycle to ride to school, and we went on holidays together. I never heard the house maid complain saying, "Why did you not send me to school, or buy a bicycle for me? Where are my new clothes, and why am I not going on holiday with the family?"

We are no longer servants, but adopted as sons and daughters of God. Therefore, we get to experience and enjoy all the benefits of God's family. You might not have a good relationship with your biological parents and find it difficult to reconcile how God can be any different. Let me reassure you that God is a good Father. He has many promises for you.

The enemy might be whispering in your ear that God cannot choose you because of what you did, or who you used to be, but let me introduce you to a few Bible characters that could have bought into the lie of the enemy:

Moses—a murderer, and he stammered

Samson—he could not say "No" to Delilah

David—an adulterer and murderer

Rahab—a prostitute

Peter—betrayer of the Lord Jesus Christ

Paul—persecutor of the Church.

God chooses the least likely to do great things. In 1 Corinthians 1:26-29, it says, "For consider your calling, brothers: not many of you were wise according to worldly standards, not many were powerful, not many were of noble birth. But God chose what is foolish in the world to shame the wise; God chose what is weak in the world to shame the strong; God chose what is low and despised in the world, even things that are not, to bring to nothing things that are, so that no human being might boast in the presence of God."

Just like Queen Esther in the Bible was chosen by the King, her status changed overnight, and she began to live like a queen in the Kings Palace. You have been chosen by the King—

walk as a prince or princess and start enjoying the benefits of His Kingdom. You did not choose Him. He chose you first and you love Him because He loved you first. You are adopted into the family of God. Walk as the son or daughter of the King.

DAY 5   DECLARATIONS

I am chosen by God
I am adopted by God
God is my Father
I am loved by God
I am special to God
I am who God says I am

PRAYER

Dear Heavenly Father, thank You for choosing me, loving me and adopting me into Your family. I ask You to help me to walk as a son/daughter of the King and not to settle for anything less. I receive all the promises in Your Word. In Jesus' name. Amen.

NOTES

Chapter 6

YOU ARE WONDERFULLY AND FEARFULLY MADE

Creation began in Genesis 1:1. The last verse of chapter 1 states, "And God saw everything that he had made, and behold, it was very good. And there was evening and there was morning, the sixth day."

Man was created on day 6. God looked at everything He had created, including man, and He said it was all "Very Good." Psalm 139:14 says, "I praise you, for I am fearfully and wonderfully made. Wonderful are your works; my soul knows it very well."

These scriptures should erase any negative words or any doubt you might have about yourself. When God created you He made you wonderful. He was pleased with His creation and He said it is very good.

You need to personalize this and say, "I am wonderfully and fearfully made, and my Maker says I am very good." You are valuable to God. His word tells you in Mathew chapter 28: 25-30, "Therefore I tell you, do not worry about your life, what you will eat or drink; or about your body, what you will wear. Is not life more than food, and the body more than clothes? Look at the birds of the air; they do not sow or reap or store away in barns, and yet your heavenly Father feeds them. Are you not much more valuable than they? Can any one of you by worrying add a single hour to your life? And why do you worry about clothes? See how the flowers of the field grow. They do not labor or spin. Yet I tell you that not even Solomon in all his splendor was dressed like one of these. If that is how God clothes the grass of the field, which is here today and tomorrow is thrown into the fire, will he not much more clothe you—you of little faith?"

Sometimes, people worry about clothing, food, or the future. Here the Word of God is telling you how God cares for the flowers in the field. He clothes the grass in the field. If He cares so much for the plants He created, how much more does He care for you, who is created in His image and His likeness?

God is perfect, and He does everything perfectly. He would never make a bad copy of Himself. Genesis 1:26a says, "Then God said, 'Let us make man in our image, after our likeness.'"

Who told you that you are not beautiful enough, or that you are ugly or undesirable? That person is a liar because your Creator declares otherwise. In the Book of Psalms, chapter 139:13, 14 says, "You alone created my inner being. You knitted me together inside my mother. I will give thanks to you because I have been so amazingly and miraculously made. Your works are miraculous, and my soul is fully aware of this."

God knitted you together in your mother's womb. Hence, the way you are is how God made you to be, even before you entered this Earth. Why should someone else, who is also a creation of God, make you feel inferior or less than themselves? Why should you buy into the standard portrayed by the social media? They portray a certain kind of beauty that disqualifies you, especially if you have not gone through plastic surgery, botox, or you aren't a size zero, or have a certain hair color or length. They judge your height and figure and countless other physical traits against their standards.

Quit trying to measure yourself against airbrushed models. The UK Daily mail quoted model Miranda Kerr: "The 30-year-old supermodel opened up to Cosmopolitan Magazine about how the pressures of the modelling industry have made it difficult in the past to find self-esteem and balance in her life." She told them that, "Models are some of the most insecure people I've ever met," she said. "They're constantly being told they're not good enough. You've really got to practice loving yourself."

These models don't see themselves as beautiful, even though the world looks to them for a standard. Why? It is because their standard is not in who God says they are, but in what people, magazines, or surveys tell them. The root of this deception is from the enemy of their soul.

The parable of the Lost Sheep tells us in Mathew 18:4-7, "Suppose one of you has a hundred sheep and loses one of them, doesn't he leave the ninety-nine in the open country and go after the lost sheep until he finds it? And when he finds it, he joyfully puts it on his shoulders and goes home. Then he calls his friends and neighbors together and says, 'Rejoice with me; I have found my lost sheep.' I tell you that in the same way there will be more rejoicing in heaven over one sinner who repents than over ninety-nine righteous persons who do not need to repent."

You are important to God. The shepherd in this parable did not say, "I have ninety nine sheep one will not make a lot of difference." He went out to look for the one because it was as valuable to Him as the rest of the flock. That is how God sees you, as a valuable sheep. He is willing to leave the rest to come and find you, because you are His creation and He loves you.

Stop seeing yourself as just a number among millions of people on this Earth. God loves you and sees you as an individual. He knows the number of hairs on your head according to Luke 12:7. Imagine that! He knows you and cares for you that much.

Psalm 139:2-4 says, "You know when I sit down or stand up. You know my thoughts even when I'm far away. You see me when I travel and when I rest at home. You know everything I do. You know what I am going to say even before I say it, LORD." God is always mindful of you. He is watching over you, wherever you are. The Bible says in Hebrews 13:5 that, "He will never leave you nor forsake you." This is how valuable you are to the almighty God.

You are never alone. Know that God is watching over you every minute of the day. Rest in His love and His care for you. Know that you are wonderfully and fearfully made by Him, and you are valuable to Him. When you are going through any difficult or challenging situations call unto God for He is near to you and always watching over you.

SOURCE: CONFIDENT
Read more: http://www.dailymail.co.uk/femail/article-2440134/Miranda-Kerr-Models-insecure-people-Ive-met.html#ixzz4k7UNe5nl

DAY 6   DECLARATIONS

I am wonderfully and fearfully made
I am valuable to God
God knows the number of hairs on my head
God said He will never leave me nor forsake me

PRAYER

Dear Heavenly Father, thank You for creating me in Your image. Forgive me for not seeing myself as You see me. I thank You for always being with me and never forsaking me. I ask You to help me to walk in the confidence of who I am in Your Word. In Jesus' name, Amen.

NOTES

_____
_____
_____
_____
_____
_____
_____
_____
_____
_____
_____
_____
_____
_____
_____
_____
_____
_____
_____

Chapter 7

YOU ARE EMPOWERED BY GOD

I would like to congratulate you for reaching day seven. Let me assure you that the Word of God on these pages is powerful and is full of life. Isaiah 55:11 says, "So shall my word be that goes out from my mouth; it shall not return to me empty, but it shall accomplish that which I purpose, and shall succeed in the thing for which I sent it."

Now that you know you are:

1. Loved by God
2. Forgiven by God
3. Restored by God
4. Accepted by God
5. Wonderfully and fearfully made by God
6. Chosen by God

You might be asking what is next? We are going to look at the story of David and Goliath in the Bible.

The Philistine army had gathered for war against Israel. The two armies faced each other, camping for battle on opposite sides of a steep valley. Goliath, a Philistine giant measuring over nine feet tall and wearing full armor, came out each day for forty days, mocking and challenging the Israelites to fight. Saul, the King of Israel, and the whole army were terrified of Goliath.

One day, David, the youngest son of Jesse, was sent to the battle lines by his father to bring back news of his brothers.

David was just a teenager at the time. While there, David heard Goliath shouting his daily defiance, and he saw the great fear stirred within the men of Israel. David responded, "Who is this uncircumcised Philistine that he should defy the armies of God?"

So, David volunteered to fight Goliath. It took some persuasion, but King Saul finally agreed to let him fight against the giant. Dressed in his simple tunic, carrying his shepherd's staff, sling, and a pouch full of stones, David approached Goliath. The giant cursed at him, hurling threats and insults.

David said to the Philistine, "You come against me with sword and spear and javelin, but I come against you in the name of the Lord Almighty, the God of the armies of Israel, whom you have defied ... today I will give the carcasses of the Philistine army to the birds of the air ... and the whole world will know that there is a God in Israel ... it is not by sword or spear that the Lord saves; for the battle is the Lord's, and He will give all of you into our hands" (1 Samuel 17:45-47).

As Goliath moved in for the kill, David reached into his bag and slung one of his stones at Goliath's head. Finding a hole in the armor, the stone sank into the giant's forehead, and he fell face down on the ground.

David then took Goliath's sword, killed him and cut off his head. When the Philistines saw that their hero was dead, they turned and ran. The Israelites pursued, chasing and killing them, plundering their camp.

Why did they wait 40 days to begin the battle? There were several reasons. Everyone was afraid of Goliath. He seemed invincible. Not even King Saul, the tallest man in Israel, had stepped out to fight him. Also, the sides of the valley were very steep. Whoever made the first move would have a strong disadvantage and probably suffer great loss. Both sides were waiting for the other to attack first.

David chose not to wear the King's armor because it felt cumbersome and unfamiliar. David was comfortable with his simple sling, a weapon he was skilled at using. God will use the unique skills He's already placed in your hands, so don't worry about "wearing the King's armor." Just be yourself and use the familiar gifts and talents God has given you. He will work miracles through you.

David's faith in God caused him to look at the giant from a different perspective. Goliath was merely a mortal man defying an all-powerful God. David looked at the battle from God's point of view. If we look at giant problems and impossible situations from God's perspective, we will realize that God will fight for us and with us. When we put things in proper perspective, we see more clearly, and we can fight more effectively.

When the giant criticized, insulted, and threatened the Israelites, David didn't stop or even waver. Everyone else cowered in fear, but David ran to the battle. He knew that action needed to be taken. David did the right thing in spite of discouraging insults and fearful threats. Only God's opinion mattered to David.

David spent time with God as a shepherd. He would sing hymns and psalms to the Lord. David had a relationship with

God, and he knew who he was in God. While the whole army of Israel was ready to run back home, David took up the challenge to fight. David knew he was not alone, with God's help he had killed a bear and a lion. He knew that he was empowered by God to overcome this Philistine Giant.

Like David, you are empowered by God to fulfill the plans and the purpose He has for your life. You are empowered by God to be a good mother, father, sister, brother, husband, wife. You are empowered by God in your career; you are empowered by God to do what you have to do on a daily basis. The Bible says in Philippians 4:13, "I can do all things through him who strengthens me."

You can do all things through Christ. He is the One Who strengthens you. David went to the battle knowing he was not going in his own strength. As you continue your journey after these seven days, you will be faced with people or situations that will try to discourage you and make you lose your identity and confidence in Christ.

David's brothers discouraged him and told him to go back home and tend the sheep. However, he refused to be intimidated, and he won the victory over the giant.

What giants are you facing? 1 Peter 5:8 teaches us to, "Be sober-minded; be watchful. Your adversary the devil prowls around like a roaring lion, seeking someone to devour." Do not let your guard down, do not become complacent in reading the Word of God and prayer. "The Word of God is a lamp unto your feet and a light unto your path" (Psalm 119:105).

This seven-day journey is designed to encourage and to help you know and understand who you are in Christ Jesus and to empower you to be who God created you to be.

You should no longer see yourself as unloved, unforgiven, unaccepted, rejected, or beyond restoration. Spread the good news of Jesus to other people, and let them also know what you have learned in these seven chapters.

If you ever face a situation that knocks you back, discourages you, or causes you to lose your identity, pick up this book and go through the seven day journey again. You can do it in one, three, five, or seven days. I encourage you to read your Bible every day. You can now listen to your Bible via various apps on your phone, tablet, PC, etc., as you drive, cook, clean, workout, or basically anywhere.

The same way you can see the road clearly with your headlights on is the same way the Word of God is a light in your life. Life can take you down some dark roads; however, you can make it through them and conquer them with the light of the Word of God.

If you do not have a relationship with God and have not accepted Him as your personal Savior, or you are not sure if you have or have not, you cannot walk in the fullness of the life He died for you to have. If you would like, please turn to the last page of this book. There you will find a prayer to help lead you into accepting Him as your Savior. He will hear you and welcome you into the Family of God.

SCRIPTURE REFERENCE:
1 Samuel 17

SOURCE:
https://www.thoughtco.com/david-and-goliath-700211

DAY 7   DECLARATIONS

I am loved by God
I am forgiven by God
I am restored by God
I am accepted by God
I am chosen by God
I am wonderfully and fearfully made
I am empowered by God to fulfill my God given purpose

PRAYER

Thank You, Lord Jesus, for this seven day journey. I ask You to give me the strength to stay in Your Word and grow in Your Word daily. I thank You for loving me, forgiving me, restoring me, accepting me, choosing me. I thank You that I am wonderfully and fearfully made and thank You for empowering me to do and to be all You created me to be.

NOTES

PRAYER OF SALVATION

Dear God, I am sorry for my sins and the life that I have lived; I need your forgiveness.

I believe that your only begotten Son Jesus Christ shed His precious blood on the cross at Calvary and died for my sins, and I am now willing to turn from my sin.

You said in Your Holy Word, Romans 10:9 that if we confess the Lord our God and believe in our hearts that God raised Jesus from the dead, we shall be saved.

I confess Jesus as Lord. With my heart, I believe and according to His Word, I am saved.

Thank You, Jesus, that your grace for saving me. Thank You for transforming my life so that I may bring glory and honor to you alone and not to myself.

Thank You, Jesus, for giving me eternal life. AMEN.

*Now, please connect with a Bible-believing church, so you will continue to be strengthened in your walk with Christ.

GOD'S PROMISES TO YOU

Philippians 4:19—God will supply all your needs
"And this same God who takes care of me will supply all your needs from his glorious riches, which have been given to us in Christ Jesus."

Romans 8:37-39—You have Victory through Christ
"No, despite all these things, overwhelming victory is ours through Christ, who loved us."

John 14:27—You have peace, do not be troubled or afraid
"I am leaving you with a gift—peace of mind and heart. And the peace I give is a gift the world cannot give. So don't be troubled or afraid."

Philippians 4:19—God will supply all your needs
"And my God will supply every need of yours according to his riches in glory in Christ Jesus."

Jeremiah 29:11—God has good plans for you
"For I know the plans I have for you, declares the Lord, plans for welfare and not for evil, to give you a future and a hope."

Psalm 37:4— God will give you the desires of your heart
"Delight yourself in the Lord, and he will give you the desires of your heart."

Romans 8:28—All things work together for your good
"And we know that for those who love God all things work together for good, for those who are called according to his purpose."

2 Peter 1:4—You are a partaker of His Divine nature
"By which he has granted to us his precious and very great promises, so that through them you may become partakers of the divine nature, having escaped from the corruption that is in the world because of sinful desire."

2 Corinthians 1:20—All God's promises are "Yes" in Him
"For all the promises of God find their Yes in him. That is why it is through him that we utter our Amen to God for his glory."

Psalm 23:1-6—God is your Shepherd
The Lord is my shepherd; I shall not want. He makes me lie down in green pastures. He leads me beside still waters. He restores my soul. He leads me in paths of righteousness for his name's sake. Even though I walk through the valley of the shadow of death, I will fear no evil, for you are with me; your rod and your staff, they comfort me. You prepare a table before me in the presence of my enemies; you anoint my head with oil; my cup overflows.

Ephesians 1:4-6—He's adopted us
"In love he predestined us for adoption as sons through Jesus Christ, according to the purpose of his will, to the praise of his glorious grace."

Galatians 4:4, 5—He's redeemed us

"But when the fullness of time had come, God sent forth his Son, born of woman, born under the law, to redeem those who were under the law, so that we might receive adoption as sons."

Romans 8:15—God is our Father

"For you did not receive the spirit of slavery to fall back into fear, but you have received the Spirit of adoption as sons, by whom we cry, 'Abba! Father!'"

ABOUT THE AUTHOR

Pastor Mags was born in Harare, Zimbabwe. She migrated to the United Kingdom in 1998, and pursued a career in Adult Nursing, specializing in cardiology and diabetes management. She is a specialist nurse, runs her own clinics and loves working in hospitals and doing charity work.

She moved to Dallas, Texas, to study at Christ For The Nations in 2014, where she received a Bachelor of Practical Ministry in Pastoral and Marketplace Ministry, as she is called to both the Church and the Marketplace. She is an ordained minister of the gospel of Jesus Christ by the Fellowship of Ministers and Churches. Mags has a certificate in Counselling from Middlesex University London. She also graduated from the Go Strategic Business and Leadership School.

She has travelled to Zimbabwe, Zambia, Kenya, Malaysia, Laos, Thailand, Myanmar, U.S.A. and Holland for ministry. She has a passion to see both men and women of all ages discover their Identity and Purpose in Christ and fulfill their God-ordained destiny. She is a mentor to many young girls and women.

Her tag line is: "You are who God says you are—not what people or circumstances have named you."

If you would like to contact Pastor Mags or to schedule her to speak at one of your conferences, go to:

pastrmags@gmail.com

Facebook – Pastor Mags (book page)

Made in the USA
Middletown, DE
30 April 2021

38044001R00045